Faith4Life

SENIOR HIGH BIBLE STUDY SERIES

IS THERE LIFE AFTER HIGH SCHOOL?

Gateway Christian Church

Group
Loveland, Colorado

Group's R.E.A.L. Guarantee to you:

This Group resource incorporates our R.E.A.L. approach to ministry—one that encourages long-term retention and life transformation. It's ministry that's:

Relational
Because learner-to-learner interaction enhances learning and builds Christian friendships.

Experiential
Because what learners experience through discussion and action sticks with them up to 9 times longer than what they simply hear or read.

Applicable
Because the aim of Christian education is to equip learners to be both hearers and doers of God's Word.

Learner-based
Because learners understand and retain more when the learning process takes into consideration how they learn best.

SENIOR HIGH BIBLE STUDY SERIES

Is There Life After High School?

Copyright © 2003 Group Publishing, Inc.

Visit our Web site: **www.grouppublishing.com**

Credits
Contributing Authors: David Adams and Michael D. Warden
Editor: Kelli B. Trujillo
Creative Development Editor: Amy Simpson
Chief Creative Officer: Joani Schultz
Copy Editor: Lyndsay E. Gerwing
Art Director: Sharon Anderson
Print Production Artist: Stephen Beer
Cover Art Director/Designer: Jeff A. Storm
Production Manager: Dodie Tipton

Unless otherwise noted, Scripture taken from the HOLY BIBLE, NEW INTERNATIONAL VERSION®. Copyright © 1973, 1978, 1984 by International Bible Society. Used by permission of Zondervan Publishing House. All rights reserved.

ISBN 0-7644-2467-X

10 9 8 7 6 5 4 3 2 1   12 11 10 09 08 07 06 05 04 03

Printed in the United States of America.

Contents

IS THERE LIFE AFTER HIGH SCHOOL?

Virtually every teenager will eventually have to face the issue of leaving home. Some "nest residents" leap out enthusiastically to the challenges of adulthood. They're excited to go out and face an unknown world on their own. Others are pushed into decisions they would never want to make on their own. "Get out there and fly!" the parent squawks with a gentle boot in the pants. The third kind of nest resident timidly peeks over the edge, sees the flurry of activity in the world below,

Independence is an exciting and terrifying proposition all rolled into one.

and retreats back into the nest, refusing to grow up and face the challenges of independence. It's very likely that all three types of students are in your youth ministry.

Independence is an exciting and terrifying proposition all rolled into one. Teenagers have so many options available to them for the future that facing life after high school can feel overwhelming. The more informed they are about what independence involves, the better equipped they'll be to handle it. And the better equipped they are to handle this life transition, the better chance they'll have at succeeding with the challenges of adulthood.

In *Is There Life After High School?* teenagers will learn that by developing integrity and seeking God's help, they can make wise choices that will positively impact their future. In the first study, they'll be challenged to think about the spiritual principles that they want to govern their decisions and life choices; teenagers will use these principles to create a personal life code.

In the second study, teenagers will be prompted to consider the practical life issues related to independence. They'll be encouraged to think beyond all of the exciting aspects of being on their own and consider the maturity that is required to successfully manage life away from home.

In the third study, students will be encouraged to seek God's help as they make choices about their future college and career options. They'll learn that there are many choices available to them, but that God should play a central role in the decision-making process.

The final study of this book will help teenagers understand the importance of maintaining relationships with their families and friends at home, even as they begin a new chapter of their lives. They'll explore what the Bible says about the importance of maintaining close relationships that can weather the changes of life.

Is There Life After High School? will help prepare teenagers to start down the road of independence. These studies will provide teenagers with a healthy boost on their journey. And while teenagers ultimately make their own decisions, your help will make that road a lot less lonely.

SENIOR HIGH BIBLE STUDY SERIES

Faith 4 Life: Senior High Bible Study Series helps teenagers take a Bible-based approach to faith and life issues. Each book in the series contains these important elements:

• Life application of Bible truth

Faith 4 Life studies help teenagers understand what the Bible says and then apply that truth to their lives.

• A relevant topic

Each Faith 4 Life book focuses on one main topic, with four studies to give your students a thorough understanding of how the Bible relates to that topic. These topics were chosen by youth leaders as the ones most relevant for senior high students.

• One point

Each study makes one point, centering on that one theme to make sure students really understand the important truth it conveys. This point is stated upfront and throughout the study.

• Simplicity

The studies are easy to use. Each contains a "Before the Study" box that outlines any advance preparation required. Each study also contains a "Study at a Glance" chart so you can quickly and easily see what supplies you'll need and what each study will involve.

• Action and interaction

Each study relies on experiential learning to help students learn what God's Word has to say. Teenagers discuss and debrief their experiences in large groups, small groups, and individual reflection.

• Reproducible handouts

Faith 4 Life books include reproducible handouts for students. No need for student books!

• Tips, tips, and more tips

Faith 4 Life studies are full of "FYI" tips for the teacher, providing extra ideas, insights into young people, and hints for making the studies go smoothly.

• Flexibility

Faith 4 Life studies include optional activities and bonus activities. Use a study as it's written, or use these options to create the study that works best for your group.

• Follow-up ideas

At the end of each book, you'll find a section called "Changed 4 Life." This section provides ideas for following up with your students to make sure the studies stick with them.

Use Faith 4 Life studies to show your teenagers how the Bible is relevant to their lives. Help them see that God can invade every area of their lives and change them in ways they can only imagine. Encourage your students to go deeper into faith—faith that will sustain them for life! Faith 4 Life, forever!

SETTING A COURSE FOR LIFE

When you get right down to it, youth ministry is all about destiny. Purpose. Helping teenagers set a straight course for their lives. We want young people to fix their spiritual sextants firmly on the Morning Star, Jesus Christ, and follow him to the end of the earth and back, without deviation or doubt.

But it's a stormy world out there. The waves can look like tsunamis. And the stars can be obscured by ominous clouds. What do we do to help our teenagers stay true to the course of life in Christ when threatening pressures assail them from every side?

Give them an inner compass to guide them through the storm. We call it *integrity*. And this study shows teenagers how to build it.

THE POINT

Living with integrity will help you follow God's course for your life.

SCRIPTURE SOURCE

Deuteronomy 5:7-21

Moses reminds God's people of the goals God has set for all who follow him.

Hebrews 12:1-2

The writer challenges Christians to look to Jesus as the focus and foundation of their lives.

THE STUDY AT A GLANCE

#1

For Starters

15 to 20 minutes

■ **SHIPS AHOY**

What students will do:
Create personalized sailboats, then swap them and tell someone what makes him or her special.

SUPPLIES:
- ❏ paper
- ❏ cardboard
- ❏ straws
- ❏ thread or yarn
- ❏ assorted craft items
- ❏ markers
- ❏ tape
- ❏ scissors

■ **BONUS ACTIVITY**
up to 5 minutes

What students will do:
Skip ahead and experience what the very end of the study will be like, then discuss what it feels like to move into the future unprepared.

SUPPLIES:
- ❏ paper
- ❏ pencils

#2

Bible Truth

25 to 30 minutes

■ **CHECKING THE SAIL**

What students will do:
Creatively discuss the roles they play in life, then create sails to represent lifetime goals.

SUPPLIES:
- ❏ Bibles
- ❏ paper
- ❏ markers
- ❏ tape
- ❏ newsprint
- ❏ scissors

#3

Life Application

5 to 10 minutes

■ **SETTING A COURSE**

What students will do:
Commit to working with a team to create one overall personal mission statement for each person in the group.

SUPPLIES:
- ❏ "My Life Code" handouts (p. 17)
- ❏ pencils

There are several ways you can help teenagers design and create their sailboats. For example, you might consider building one yourself before the study and having it ready to show to teenagers as an example. Or if you have access to pictures of sailboats (in a calendar, magazine, or book), bring them in for teenagers to look at.

Roam the room while teenagers work, and point out any creative ideas you see teenagers using that might help your students learn from each other.

BEFORE THE STUDY

Before the study, set out paper, cardboard, markers, tape, scissors, newsprint, and other craft supplies. Also, make enough copies of the "My Life Code" handout (p. 17) so that each student can have one.

FOR STARTERS

15 to 20 minutes

SHIPS AHOY

Say: There are lots of challenges awaiting you as you look ahead toward life after high school. You'll be faced with many tough choices and encounter many positive opportunities. Your journey into adulthood can be best navigated if you live with integrity—if you live by a personal life code that governs your actions.

To start our odyssey toward creating a personal life code, we're going to create personalized sailboats to help us discover just what kind of people we are.

Set out paper, cardboard, straws, thread or yarn, scissors, tape, markers, and as many other assorted craft items as you can find (such as cloth scraps, pipe cleaners, craft sticks, toothpicks, rubber bands, paper clips, and pencils). Have teenagers use the supplies to design and create their own sailboats. Tell teenagers they don't have to make anything elaborate, just something that definitely has sails. Encourage teenagers to work together as they like, but remind them that each person needs to have his or her own sailboat.

When teenagers have completed their sailboats, have them form pairs and explain to their partners at least three ways their sailboats represent them.

Then have partners switch sailboats. Call everyone together in a circle and **say:**

Living with integrity will help you follow God's ◀**THE POINT** course for your life. God wants us to have integrity— to live by his laws and guidelines. But that doesn't mean we'll all be alike. Just look at the variety of sailboats we have! Each of us is unique and special to God. Having integrity means discovering who God made *you* to be, then living that out to the best of your ability.

If you have more than twelve people in your group, you might consider forming two or more "sharing" circles instead of just one.

Let's go around the circle and each tell one unique quality about the boat you're holding. Then tell how that unique quality makes your partner special.

Starting with the person on your right, go around the circle and allow teenagers to share. After everyone has shared, have teenagers return sailboats to the owners. Then have teenagers set their boats on the floor and join hands for prayer.

Pray: **Lord, thank you for creating each of us with such an incredible and unique beauty. Thank you for making everyone in this room special in your eyes. In the remaining time we have together, I ask that you help each of us discover the unique person you created us to be so that we can be true to ourselves and to you. In Jesus' name, amen.**

Since some of your teenagers might not know what the word *integrity* means, you can bring them up to speed by reading aloud this definition from *Webster's New World College Dictionary:* "the quality or state of being of sound moral principle; uprightness, honesty, and sincerity."

► BONUS ACTIVITY

up to 5 minutes

If you have time, use this idea to begin the "Ships Ahoy" activity. What you'll do here is "skip ahead" to the conclusion of the lesson and pretend that the study is over. Teenagers will soon realize that they aren't prepared to create their own personal mission statements yet and will consider how this same type of unpreparedness can negatively affect them in life.

As teenagers arrive, have them form groups of four, and give each group paper and pencils. Once everyone has arrived, **say:**

> **We've had a great study today! I'm so glad each of you has had the opportunity to think about who you really want to be in life. Now I want you to work with your group to create a personal mission statement for each person in your group. Remember, the statement should take into account all the roles you play in life. When everyone has finished, we'll close with prayer. OK, you can get started.**

Wait about a minute while teenagers try to follow your instructions. Then stop the activity, and ask teenagers to **discuss** these questions in their groups:

> ● **Is anything bothering you about this activity? If so, what?**
> ● **Do you feel ready to do the closing activity for the study? Why or why not?**
> ● **How is that feeling like how it feels to move into your future unprepared?**
> ● **Do you think it's important to have a sense of purpose in life? Why or why not?**

Call groups together and **say:**

> **I decided to "begin with the end" today to illustrate why it's important to make decisions now about the kind of person you want to be, because the decisions you make today will shape your destiny—the "end" of your life's story.**
>
> **Living a personal "code" builds integrity and firmly sets the course of your life so that things like peer pressure, worries, and personal conflicts won't ever keep you from reaching your potential in Christ.**
>
> **Today we're going to help each other develop personal codes to live by so that we can discover the power integrity brings to our lives.**

CHECKING THE SAIL

Say: Before you can set a course for the future, you have to know where you are. Let's take some time to discover who we are right now by looking at the roles we play in our lives.

Have teenagers form groups of four or fewer, and give each group paper, scissors, markers, and tape. Then **say:**

Take a sheet of paper and secretly write on it all the roles you play in life. For example, you're playing the role of a student right now. You also play roles in your family, at school, at work, with your friends—the list goes on. Try to list at least five roles you play, but don't list more than ten. And don't let any of your group members see your list yet.

While teenagers work, tape a sheet of newsprint to the wall, and list all the roles *you* play in life, to provide teenagers with an example of what kind of information you're looking for.

When teenagers have finished, **say:**

Now you're going to tell your fellow group members about the roles you wrote down. But you're not going to tell them in the ordinary way. Instead, you're going to draw pictures that illustrate each of the roles you wrote down. And there's a catch: You have to keep your eyes closed while you draw.

Distribute additional paper to teenagers, then have teenagers close their eyes and draw illustrations that represent each of the roles they wrote down. When everyone has finished, have group members take turns showing their "art" and letting the group guess the role each drawing illustrates.

When all the roles have been discovered, **ask:**

● What was difficult about this activity?

● How is drawing with your eyes closed like trying to live without a clear sense of who you are?

● How can developing a personal life code help you live with integrity and follow God's course for your life? ⟨THE POINT

● How can understanding the roles you play in life help you develop a personal life code?

Say: The roles you play in life can be like the sails on your sailboat. When all the sails are working together, the boat can catch more wind and travel faster toward your goal. But when the sails are turned in different directions, the boat can flounder in the water and never get anywhere. That's why understanding the roles you play in life can be so important.

Have teenagers find a partner and **discuss** these questions:

- Are there any roles you play in life that you think aren't good for you? Explain.
- Are there any roles you don't have that you think would be good for you to have? Explain.

Have teenagers change their lists of roles based on their responses to these questions by adding roles they think would benefit them and eliminating roles that don't.

Say: Now that we all have a working list of roles we play in life, I want you each to use the supplies I gave you to create a new sail for your boat that lists a lifetime goal for each of the roles on your list. For example, if one of your roles is "son" or "daughter," your lifetime goal for that role could be something like, "I want to be known as someone who always honored my parents."

To help teenagers create their goals, have them read together Hebrews 12:1-2 and Deuteronomy 5:7-21. **Ask:**

- How can living by God's guidelines point you in the right direction in life? Share an example.
- How is life like a race?
- How is focusing on Jesus like focusing on a "finish line"?

Invite students to reread both passages on their own, then **say:**

Use these passages as a guide for creating your goals.

As teenagers complete their sails, have them attach the sails to their boats and explain their goals to their group members. Encourage group members to discuss their goals within their groups by sharing what they like about each other's goals and making suggestions for how the goals could be strengthened.

When groups have finished, **say:**

Congratulations! You're now well on your way to creating a personal life code. Living with integrity  will help you follow God's course for your life. Setting goals like these can help you do that in a powerful way.

---

*FYI

If some teenagers have trouble coming up with lifetime goals for their roles, suggest they begin writing their goals with the phrase, "I want to be known as someone who..." This will help teenagers think through what's most important to them concerning each role on their lists.

As an added help to teenagers, provide them with a copy of your own lifetime goals for each of the roles you play in life.

LIFE APPLICATION

SETTING A COURSE

Say: Now you're ready to embark on the final stage of our process: creating an overall "life code" based on all the roles you identified. Creating a life code will help you live with integrity and follow God's course for your life. But creating a life code is no small task, and it's going to take each of you some time and thought to create one for yourself that both challenges you and pleases God. But don't worry. You don't have to do it alone. Your friends are going to help you.

Distribute pencils and copies of the "My Life Code" handout.

Say: This handout is designed to be a guide to help you create an overall personal life code based on all the discoveries we've made so far. After looking over the handout, I want you to work with your group to pick a time and place to meet so you can work together to create a personal life code for each person in your group.

Doing this important task with your group is important for two reasons. First, you can benefit from each other's input and help each other create the best life code possible. And second, once your life codes are complete, you can help each other stick to them in the coming year.

Have teenagers follow the instructions in Part 1 of the handout. When they've finished, have them pray together for each individual in their group, asking God to help him or her be faithful to building integrity by setting a solid course for his or her life.

FYI

Create a personal life code? My teenagers? You must be kidding! They don't even know what they want to do *tomorrow*. How can I expect them to decide what they're going to be like for the rest of their lives?

The teenage years are fickle. We all know that. A young person's personality can change as quickly as the weather and without warning. But when it comes to issues of personal character—that is, helping teenagers decide what kind of people they *want* to be—their outlook becomes much more consistent. Most of your teenagers probably have some idea of the type of people they want to become, even if they don't quite know how to get there yet.

Creating a personal life code can help teenagers recognize the spiritual principles that lead to true success in life. And even if they don't follow their code perfectly, just having created it can help build within your teenagers a sense of purpose and direction.

• MY LIFE CODE •

PART 1

As a group, decide on a time and place to meet to create your own personal life code. After your initial meeting, you may want to get together again a week or so later to make any additional changes you think would strengthen your life code.

When we'll meet: •••

Where we'll meet: •••

Remember to bring with you this handout, your sailboat, your Bible, and a pencil! ➤ •

➤ PART 2

"Therefore, since we are surrounded by such a great cloud of witnesses, let us throw off everything that hinders and the sin that so easily entangles, and let us run with perseverance the race marked out for us. Let us fix our eyes on Jesus, the author and perfecter of our faith, who for the joy set before him endured the cross, scorning its shame, and sat down at the right hand of the throne of God" (Hebrews 12:1-2).

Follow the instructions below, and work with your group to create your own personal life code.

 1. Read through the Scripture passage above, and tell the group at least three things about the passage that can help you create a life code that would please God.

 2. Read through the goals you created during the study, then use them to guide you as you write an answer to this question: "What do you want people to remember about you after you die?"

3. Use the information above, along with your goals from the study, to create a personal life code on the back of this sheet. Try to keep your code brief—no more than ten or twelve lines long.

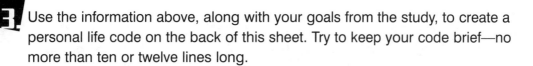

READY FOR INDEPENDENCE?

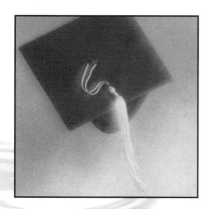

Independence seems to be every teenager's dream. Most teenagers count the days until they get to make their own decisions or "live their own lives." Unfortunately, many teenagers don't realize how difficult independence is until they're suddenly on their own. And many have problems dealing with independence. We can help ease the stress of this important life transition by preparing young people for life after high school.

THE POINT

Independence requires wisdom and maturity.

SCRIPTURE SOURCE

Proverbs 3:1-13
The writer explains the virtues of wisdom.

1 Corinthians 13:9-12
Paul writes about how maturity changes one's perspective on things.

THE STUDY AT A GLANCE

#1

For Starters
up to 15 minutes

■ **ARE YOU READY?**

What students will do:
Take a quiz to see if they're really ready for independence.

SUPPLIES:
❑ "Are You Ready?" hand-outs (p. 27)
❑ pencils

■ **OPTIONAL ACTIVITY**
10 to 15 minutes

What students will do:
Clean up a messy room and consider what it is really like to live on one's own.

SUPPLIES:
❑ dirty clothes
❑ dirty dishes
❑ ironing board

#2

Bible Truth
20 to 30 minutes

■ **WHEN I GROW UP**

What students will do:
Discuss the differences between childhood and adulthood.

SUPPLIES:
❑ tape
❑ newsprint
❑ markers
❑ Bibles
❑ modeling clay
❑ pencils

#3

Life Application
5 to 10 minutes

■ **TOY BOX**

What students will do:
Lay down childhood toys.

SUPPLIES:
❑ paper
❑ pencils
❑ pocket calendar
❑ cell phone, or other adult "toy"

BEFORE THE STUDY

Before the study, make enough photocopies of the "Are You Ready?" handout (p. 27) so that each student can have one. If you're doing the "Optional Activity," mess up your meeting room so that it looks like a typical disorganized dorm room or apartment. Set out newsprint, markers, modeling clay, and pens or pencils. Also, select an adult "toy," such as a hand-held personal digital assistant, cell phone, or organizer.

Add a dose of fun to this activity by making it a game. After students have filled out the quiz and formed small groups, challenge them to try to guess, one at a time, which answers the teenagers in their group selected. This will be a great way to help the students get to know each other better.

Teenagers can greatly benefit from hearing how others have "made it" through the adolescent years to become successful adults. Consider taking a few minutes to share your own journey with your students. What were some of your fears about growing up? What did you look forward to? What were the greatest challenges about living on your own? What were the best things about your new independence? What lessons did you learn from your mistakes?

FOR STARTERS

up to 15 minutes

ARE YOU READY?

Give each teenager a photocopy of the "Are You Ready?" handout (p. 27) and a pencil. Invite students to take some time filling out the quiz. When they've finished, have them form groups of three and take turns sharing their answers. Prompt teenagers to share their reasons for each answer.

Then have teenagers form a circle, and **ask:**

- **Did this quiz reveal anything to you about your readiness to leave home? Explain.**

- **Is it possible to be fully prepared to leave home? Why or why not?**

- **How do you think your faith will affect the things that happen to you when you leave home?**

- **What will be the best parts of independence?**

- **What will be the worst parts?**

- **What pressures do you think you'll face that you don't face now?**

Say: It's easy to say we're ready for independence, but it's not so easy to actually be prepared for what lies ahead. Independence requires wisdom and maturity. Today we'll explore some of the issues involved in breaking away from parents and being on your own.

OPTIONAL ACTIVITY

Instead of the "Are You Ready?" activity, try this optional activity. Before the lesson, mess up your meeting room. Toss dirty clothes around the room, lay dirty dishes around, set up an ironing board, and mess up the furniture and other things to give the appearance of a messy apartment.

Have teenagers form two teams to compete in a contest, and identify teams as Team 1 and Team 2. **Say:**

> **We're going to have a contest between these two teams. Team members, pretend you're roommates and you've just gotten home from work. Look around—this is your apartment. Unfortunately, you have a party starting at your place in a few minutes, and you aren't ready for it. Each team will have two minutes to straighten up this place before guests arrive. Then I'll rate each team on your preparedness on a scale of one to ten.**

> **We'll start with Team 1. You can do anything you want to get this room ready in two minutes, but keep everything in this room.**

On "go," start timing the first team. While they're working on cleaning up, try some tricks such as "calling" them on the phone, sending in a "neighbor" from the other team to borrow something, or having a "guest" arrive early. When the two minutes are up, rate the preparedness of the room on a scale of one to ten. Don't be too generous with your ranking. Find specifics that aren't perfect and deduct points for those items.

Mess up the room again, and have Team 2 attempt to clean the room. Once again, interrupt the team's efforts with "visitors" and "guests" arriving early.

After scoring the second team, **ask:**

- **How did you feel during this activity?**
- **How is this like the feeling teenagers might have when they're living on their own?**
- **How is this activity like or unlike independent living? Explain.**
- **What new pressures did you feel in this activity that you don't feel now while you're living at home?**
- **What are some pressures adults have that teenagers living at home don't have?**

Say: There is no perfect time for becoming independent. No matter when you're on your own, you'll probably discover many things you wish you'd already learned. But the key to successfully developing your independence is in putting away childish things and learning to be responsible. **Independence requires wisdom and maturity.** ◀THE POINT

Have everyone work together to straighten up the room.

20 to 30 minutes

WHEN I GROW UP

Tape two large sheets of newsprint to the wall. Write the heading "When I was a child..." on one newsprint sheet and "But when I became an adult..." on the other.

Have students form groups of four, and invite one volunteer in each group to read aloud 1 Corinthians 13:9-12 while the other students read along in their Bibles. **Ask:**

- **Can you relate to what Paul is saying? Explain.**
- **How have you changed since you were a young child? Give specific examples.**
- **How do you expect to change as you become an adult?**
- **What does it mean to become "mature"?**

When small groups have finished discussing, have students each write a phrase or draw a picture on each piece of newsprint about a major advantage or disadvantage of that time of life. For example, on the "When I was a child..." newsprint, someone might write, "Children don't have many responsibilities" or "Children can't do much on their own." On the "But when I became an adult..." newsprint, someone might write, "Adults can do whatever they want" or "Adults have too many bills to pay."

After everyone has finished, have students return to their groups of four, and ask them to explain any pictures or phrases they put on the newsprint.

Then **ask:**

- **Which statements or drawings on each sign mean the most to you? Explain.**
- **How different is adulthood from childhood? Explain.**
- **If you could be an adult or a child for the rest of your life, which would you choose? Explain.**

Invite students to form one large group, and give each teenager a lump of modeling clay and a pencil. Have each teenager shape his or her clay into a heart. Invite several volunteers to read aloud Proverbs 3:1-13, taking turns reading one verse at a time. As the Scripture is read, have each teenager write one word on his or her heart that captures this Scripture's message. For example, teenagers might write "wisdom," "understanding," or "God." When teenagers have finished, have them bring their clay heart symbols to the front and set them all together on display.

Ask:

- What advice does this passage give to people who are becoming independent?

- How would you define *wisdom* in your own words?

- When does an adult need wisdom? Give some practical examples.

- What frightens you most about becoming an adult?

- What excites you most about becoming independent?

Say: It's a long journey from childhood to adulthood, but you've already come much of the distance in the past few years. Independence requires wisdom and maturity. There are specific things you can do to become more responsible and grow in maturity.

LIFE APPLICATION

TOY BOX

Give each teenager a sheet of paper and a pencil. Have him or her draw a favorite childhood toy, such as a doll or a model car. After everyone has finished drawing, **say:**

> **Growing up can be very scary. We have to overcome our fears and face the challenge of independence  with wisdom and maturity. Sometimes growing up means we give up childish habits. We begin making wise decisions in a mature way.**

THE POINT

Instruct teenagers to think about something they need to "grow out of" in order to become a wise and mature person, ready for independence. Encourage them to each write a word, letter, or symbol on their toys to represent that part of their lives.

> **Say: If you're committed to growing, come to the front of the room and place your childhood toy beside an adult "toy."**

On a table at the front of the room, lay an adult toy, such as a handheld personal digital assistant or cell phone. Allow time for teenagers to come to the front of the room and leave their drawings beside the adult toy.

Have teenagers form pairs, and have each partner take a turn completing the following sentence: "For me, becoming an adult means..."

Then invite volunteers to tell the whole group how they completed the sentence.

ARE YOU READY?

For each numbered item, circle the answer that most closely matches your own.

1. The first thing I need to get when I leave home is

a. a job.
b. a place to live.
c. a roommate.
d. a car.
e. a scholarship.

2. I plan to visit my parents

a. every week.
b. once a month.
c. every day.
d. once a semester.
e. on holidays only.
f. never.
g. only when there's nowhere else to go.

3. I'll visit my parents for

a. money.
b. a place to do laundry.
c. food.
d. moral support.
e. a place to hide.

4. On the first Sunday after I move out, I plan to

a. go to my home church.
b. start at a new church.
c. sleep very late.
d. figure out what to do at the time.

5. If I'm forced to live with roommates who I don't already know, the first question I want answered is

a. can they afford to live here?
b. where do they go to church?
c. are they trustworthy?
d. what kind of friends do they have?
e. what kind of bad habits do they have?

6. The first question I'll ask about a place I'm thinking of moving into is

a. does it have roaches?
b. is it in a safe neighborhood?
c. how much does it cost?
d. are the utilities expensive?
e. does it have cable TV?
f. how far is it from work or school?
g. do they take pets?

7. The one thing I'll miss the most when I move out is

a. my parents and family.
b. my friends.
c. the food.
d. having money.
e. a sense of security.
f. my church.

8. The one thing I'll miss the least when I leave home is

a. my parents and family.
b. the food.
c. the lack of privacy.
d. my church.
e. a curfew.

CHOICES, CHOICES, CHOICES!

- **What kind of job do you want?**
- **Where are you going to go to college?**
- **What will you major in?**

Teenagers are familiar with these questions and with the stress that accompanies them. As teenagers near graduation, they have some serious choices to make, and the pressure can often feel overwhelming!

The good news is that God can give them the wisdom they need to make those difficult choices. God has given them unique talents and interests, and he can use those talents for good in their chosen careers.

Use this study to help teenagers begin thinking more seriously about their future choices—and help them focus on God in the process.

THE POINT

God can help you make wise choices about your future.

SCRIPTURE SOURCE

Genesis 49:1-28
Jacob blesses each of his sons, describing their different personalities and lifestyle choices.

Ephesians 2:8-10
Paul writes that God has good things planned for us to do.

Proverbs 2:6
The writer explains that God provides wisdom to those who seek it.

THE STUDY AT A GLANCE

#1

For Starters
10 to 15 minutes

■ **OPTION PLAY**

What students will do:
Play a game about career and lifestyle choices.

SUPPLIES:
❑ shoe boxes
❑ tape
❑ markers
❑ scissors
❑ "Life Points" handouts (p. 36)
❑ paper
❑ pencils

■ **BONUS ACTIVITY**
5 to 10 minutes

What students will do:
Make choices about fruit they want to eat.

SUPPLIES:
❑ basket
❑ fruit

#2

Bible Truth
20 to 25 minutes

■ **JOB HUNT**

What students will do:
Create "position wanted" ads for Bible characters.

SUPPLIES:
❑ Bibles
❑ paper
❑ pencils

#3

Life Application
15 to 20 minutes

■ **DECISION TIME**

What students will do:
Use a handout to think through the choices they are facing.

SUPPLIES:
❑ Bible
❑ "Decision Time" hand-outs (p. 37)
❑ pencils
❑ newsprint banner
❑ marker

BEFORE THE STUDY

Before the study, collect several shoe boxes and set them out, along with tape, makers, and scissors. Make enough photocopies of the "Life Points" handout (p. 36) so that each group of four can have one. You'll also need to make one copy of the "Decision Time" handout (p. 37) for each student. If you decide to do the "Bonus Activity," you'll need a variety of types of fruit, one fruit per student. Finally, tape a large newsprint banner to the wall for use in the Life Application discussion.

FOR STARTERS

10 to 15 minutes

OPTION PLAY

When teenagers arrive, have them form groups of no more than four. Give each group a shoe box, tape, a marker, scissors, and a photocopy of the "Life Points" handout (p. 36). Give each person a sheet of paper and a pencil.

Have each group use its shoe box, tape, marker, and scissors to create a die (see the illustration in the margin). They'll have to cut and tape the box to make it square. Be sure groups write the numbers one through six on their dice.

Tell teenagers they're going to play a game that represents their future life. The object of the game is to finish with the most points: the more points gained, the more fulfilling the life. Have groups follow the rules on their "Life Points" handouts to play the game.

Have teenagers take turns rolling their group's die and recording their roll's point value. Whenever someone rolls a number worth more than fifty points, have group members say, "Ding, ding, ding," like a bell. For anything fifty points or lower, have group members make a noise like a buzzer. Encourage students to keep track of the points and categories they each received.

After each group plays four rounds, bring groups together and have teenagers compare point totals.

Then **ask:**

- **How did you feel as you played this game? Explain.**

- **How is this like or unlike the way people feel about their roles in real life? Explain.**

- **How accurately do the point values reflect real life? Explain.**

*FYI

If you're short on time, create the large shoe-box dice before the lesson or use regular playing dice.

- What will it take to make you happy in the future?
- How has this game affected the way you see the choices you could make after you graduate?
- Of all the things you could do after you graduate, what is the *last* thing you want to do?

Say: None of these things make people better than others, but some lifestyles are more fulfilling than others. You may have a great career but work eighty hours a week. Soon, you'll be overworked, exhausted, and unfulfilled. Or you may have a not-so-good job but a great family life that fulfills you. Making a good choice for what you'll do after high school isn't easy. But you can be assured that there are many good choices to be made. God can help you make wise choices **THE POINT** about your future. Let's explore a Bible passage to see the variety of roles people can choose in life.

>> BONUS ACTIVITY

If you have time, try this bonus activity before "Option Play." Have teenagers sit in a circle. Set a basket of a variety of fruit in the center of the circle. **Say:**

> I've brought enough fruit for everyone to have one piece, but there are limited numbers of each fruit. Choose the fruit you want. If someone chooses the fruit you want, you may choose another fruit from the basket or take someone else's fruit.

Go around the circle, and have each teenager choose a piece of fruit. After everyone has a piece of fruit, allow one more opportunity for teenagers to trade with someone else.

Then **ask:**

- **How did you feel during this activity?**
- **How is this experience like or unlike the choices you'll have to make after graduation?**
- **How do you feel when you think about choosing a future career?**

Say: For many people, choosing what to do after college is like choosing a piece of fruit from our basket. Many options look equally attractive, and it's often difficult to know exactly what you want. But ultimately your choices directly affect the end result. In order to get the end result you hope for in life, you need to make wise choices along the way. In this study, we're going to look at how you can make wise choices about your future.

20 to 25 minutes

JOB HUNT

Have teenagers form up to twelve groups. A group can be as small as one person. Assign each group one or more of Jacob's sons from Genesis 49:1-28.

Give each group a Bible, a sheet of paper for each of the sons, and a pencil. Have groups read aloud Genesis 49:1-28. After reading the Scripture, have each group create a "position wanted" ad for its sons. Tell groups to be creative, since some jobs may not be obvious. Have them include specifics about the people in their ads—for example, Reuben's ad could say, "Looking for a construction work job that can use my strength. Know how to overcome any situation. Don't relate well to authority, and lack self-control. Other than that, a great worker."

After groups have written their advertisements, have each group read its advertisement(s) aloud.

Then **ask:**

- **How difficult was it to write your ad? Explain.**

- **What connection was there between individual character qualities and the work the people did?**

- **How is this like or unlike real life?**

- **How do your personal characteristics relate to your dream career? Explain.**

Have teenagers form a circle. One by one, have them stand in the center of the circle. Have them call out character qualities they see in the person in the center and what career he or she would be good at. Remind teenagers to be positive and uplifting. For example, they may say, "Patient, a teacher"; "Kind, a doctor"; or "Helpful, a social worker."

Say: **Each of Jacob's sons lived a lifestyle that fit with his personality and the choices he made. Some of the brothers made unwise choices in life that had bad results. Others made wise choices and found success because of them. Like Jacob's sons, you can find a lifestyle that fits your personality. But you can't get where you want to go without thinking through your goals and the choices you'll need to make in order to achieve them. God can help you make wise choices to help you achieve your future goals.** ◀ **THE POINT**

Invite a student to read Proverbs 2:6, and **ask:**

- **How can you seek wisdom from God when it comes to making choices about life after graduation?**

LIFE APPLICATION

15 to 20 minutes

DECISION TIME

Invite students to form pairs and think about all of the choices a high school student needs to make when it comes to deciding to go to college, getting a job, moving out, choosing a career, and so on. Give pairs time to list the choices they've thought of on the large newsprint banner on the wall. Once all of the pairs have finished writing their questions, encourage all of the students to read the choices that their peers wrote.

> **Say:** **Choosing a career or a college is not an easy decision. There are *a lot* of choices that need to be made, and it's important to include God in the decision process.**

Give each person a photocopy of the "Decision Time" handout (p. 37) and a pencil. Have teenagers read and complete their handouts and then form groups of no more than five. Have teenagers share what they wrote on their handouts and discuss the steps it might take to reach their goals. Prompt small groups to spend time praying together for each other as they seek God's wisdom about their choices.

Then have students form a circle, and have volunteers tell what they discovered in talking about their goals.

Encourage teenagers to take their sheets home and show them to a parent or sibling.

Invite a volunteer to read aloud Ephesians 2:8-10.

> **Say:** **God has already planned good things for you to do in your life. And when it comes to all of the decisions you are facing,** you can trust God to help you **◄THE POINT** make wise choices about your future.

LIFE POINTS

Take turns rolling your homemade die and recording the point value of your roll.

Play four rounds, and then total your points.

The person in each group with the most points is the winner and gets the most happiness in life.

Round One

1—Physician=100 points
2—Teacher=75 points
3—Electrician=75 points
4—Computer technician=50 points
5—Administrative Assistant=25 points
6—Garbage collector=10 points

Round Two

1—Married, with children=100 points
2—Married, no children=75 points
3—Engaged=50 points
4—Single=50 points
5—Divorced=25 points
6—Widowed=10 points

Round Three

1—$200,000 salary=100 points
2—$100,000 salary=75 points
3—$45,000 salary=50 points
4—$20,000 salary=25 points
5—Disability pension=10 points
6—No salary=0 points

Round Four

1—40-hour work week=100 points
2—Self-employed=75 points
3—Business president=75 points
4—Part-time work=50 points
5—80-hour work week=25 points
6—Unemployed=10 points

DECISION TIME

Read and complete the following sentences.

➤ Some of the difficult decisions I'm trying to make right now about my future are...

➤ One of my goals for the future is...

➤ The steps I'll have to make to reach this goal include...

➤ If reaching my goal requires more schooling, I'll...

➤ If my dream requires getting a job after high school, I'll...

Take a moment to write a prayer to God about the decisions you are making.

➤ Dear God, right now I need your wisdom...

REMEMBERING YOUR ROOTS

Leaving home is often a difficult time for teenagers. Some students may be ready and raring to get out of the house and experience independence, while others may feel terrified. Usually, students from both groups wind up feeling distant and separated from their families once they've left home.

Teenagers can prepare themselves to become independent by looking at what breaking away is, getting in touch with their feelings about it, strengthening relationships with those who are (or will be) going through the process with them, and finding support from the people who've helped them become who they are. This study will challenge teenagers who are embarking on new lives of independence to place a high priority on maintaining their past relationships.

THE POINT

As you grow and change, it's important to stay connected to home and family.

SCRIPTURE SOURCE

Ecclesiastes 4:5-12
The writer explains the importance and benefit of close relationships.

Luke 4:14-30
This passage describes Jesus' return to his hometown and the unwelcome reception he received there.

THE STUDY AT A GLANCE

#1

For Starters
15 to 20 minutes

■ **THE UMBILICAL PROJECT**

What students will do:
Experience different degrees of independence.

SUPPLIES:
❏ "Tough Calls" handouts (p. 46)
❏ pencils

#2

Bible Truth
25 to 30 minutes

■ **THE CHILD YOU WERE**

What students will do:
List what they'd like to become and what people will remember about them.

SUPPLIES:
❏ Bibles
❏ paper
❏ pencils
❏ yarn

#3

Life Application
5 to 10 minutes

■ **THE ROOT CELLAR**

What students will do:
Consider how important their roots are.

SUPPLIES:
❏ root

■ **OPTIONAL ACTIVITY**
10 to 15 minutes

What students will do:
Write ways others have helped them.

SUPPLIES:
❏ paper
❏ pencils

FOR STARTERS

15 to 20 minutes

THE UMBILICAL PROJECT

Have teenagers form three groups. Give each group a photocopy of the "Tough Calls" handout (p. 46) and a pencil.

Say: We're going to try a little experiment. Each of your groups is to complete the "Tough Calls" handout as well as possible within ten minutes. Group 1, you'll work on this activity someplace by yourselves, and I'll send someone to get you when the time's up. (Send them to their area or room.) Group 2, you'll also be sent out alone, but you're allowed to come back to me three times between now and the end of this exercise. Each time you may only ask one question. (Send them to their area or room.) Group 3, you can work on this handout right here with me. I'll answer any questions you have during this activity.

Answer any questions Group 3 has, and work closely with these group members as they complete the handout. Give them advice and generally be too involved with the group. If anyone from Group 2 comes in and asks you for help, give them exactly what they ask for but no more. Remember to tell them how many times they've been in to see you. Only three times are allowed.

When Group 3 has completed the handout, or after about ten minutes, have the other two groups return to the room. When everyone's together, have groups read what they've written. Then explain to the whole group your role with each different group.

Ask:

● How did you feel during this activity?

- How is this like the way teenagers who are breaking away from their parents feel?

- Which group was the most independent?

- Which group had the best situation?

- How is this activity like or unlike the independence some people have from their families? Explain.

- Which level of independence or connection from this activity is most like the type of relationship you'd like to keep with your family and friends when you complete high school? Why?

- Do you want to leave home after high school? Why or why not?

- What will be the best parts about leaving home?

- What will be the toughest parts?

Say: There are different degrees of independence. Important things can happen once someone decides to leave home; people begin to grow in new ways. But their growth can actually be hindered if they totally reject or cling to their families. As you grow and **THE POINT** change, it's important to learn a healthy balance of independence and dependence as you stay connected to home and family.

BIBLE TRUTH

25 to 30 minutes

THE CHILD YOU WERE

nvite volunteers to read aloud Luke 4:14-30, then **ask:**

FYI

Some teenagers feel that they'll never change; they don't fully understand what the future may hold for them. If some of your students feel this way, it may be a good idea to share an example from your own life of a way you changed once you left home. It would also be helpful for you to share how those personal changes affected your relationships with friends and family members.

- How did the people from Jesus' hometown respond to him?

- Why do you think they rejected what Jesus claimed?

- How do you think Jesus felt when the community he grew up in rejected him?

Say: Like a lot of people, it wasn't easy for Jesus to go home after he'd left. People had memories of him as a little boy, and they had trouble accepting him as the man he had become. Since he'd left, he had changed as the power of God began to be revealed through him. His old friends couldn't accept these changes.

Ask: How important is it for you to leave home? Explain.

- Do you worry that you might not be accepted back home once you've been on your own? Why or why not?

- Do you think you'll change when you leave home? In what ways?

- What's more important, doing what you believe is right in life or meeting the expectations of your family and friends? Explain.

Distribute a sheet of paper and a pencil to each person.

Say: Think about your life as a child. In the middle of your sheet of paper, write what you would most like to become within the next ten years. Above that, make a list of about five to ten things you think people around here will remember from your childhood. For example, you might list a sports team you were on, a solo you sang in church, or a project you completed for school. Below it, write at least three things from your childhood that you wish no one would remember. For example, you might list a mistake you made in school, a time you broke something valuable, or a time you ran away from home.

After everyone has finished writing, have teenagers form pairs. Have partners share what they wrote.

Say: Each of us has grown and changed since childhood.

Likewise, each of us will grow and change in the future. **As you grow and change, it's important to stay connected to home and family.** One of the challenges of leaving home, though, is staying connected to people at home who may not understand the ways you're changing and growing.

Have pairs read Ecclesiastes 4:5-12.

Ask: ■ **What does this passage mean to you?**

■ **Do you think the observations in these verses are true to real life? Explain.**

■ **What does this passage imply about maintaining close relationships with your family and friends?**

■ **How important is it to stay "plugged in" with what's going on back home? Explain.**

■ **How can you maintain a close relationship with your family once you're on your own?**

Give each teenager a piece of thick yarn. Have teenagers peel off strands of the yarn, give the people around them each a strand, and tell one thing they appreciate about their friendship. For example, someone might say, "I appreciate the way you're always here for me" or "I appreciate the strength you give me." Tell teenagers to save a few strands of the yarn to give to family members along with words of appreciation.

Say: It's not always easy to keep in touch with family and friends once you're on your own. But you can if you maintain relationships. The relationships God has given us in our families and friends are some of the most valuable we have.

FYI

Use the yarn as an object lesson, pointing out to students the connection with Ecclesiastes 4:12b. Encourage them to think of the strength that comes from friendships as they participate in the yarn activity.

LIFE APPLICATION

5 to 10 minutes

THE ROOT CELLAR

Have teenagers form a large circle. Go around the circle with an extended tree or plant root, breaking off a piece and giving it to each person.

Say: You'll take many memories with you when you leave home. The memories you've made and the friends you have will be with you for a lifetime because they're a part of who you are—your roots in life. Each person here has provided nourishment to your roots to help you grow. As you grow and change, it's impor- **◁THE POINT** tant to stay connected to home and family.

Have each teenager turn to the person on his or her left, give the root to that person, and tell how that person has helped him or her grow.

Close with a time of prayer and prompt students to pray together in pairs. Encourage them to pray prayers of celebration as they remember their common roots. Close by asking God to help the teenagers always remember to show gratitude to him—the one who is the root of us all.

OPTIONAL ACTIVITY

10 to 15 minutes

Instead of the "Root Cellar" activity, try this optional activity.

Have teenagers form circles of no more than six. Give each teenager a sheet of paper and a pencil. Have teenagers fold their papers in half twice to make small booklets. Have teenagers write their names on their booklets and then pass them to the right, and prompt teenagers to write in each booklet one way that person has helped them grow. Continue until booklets are returned to the original owners.

When the booklets have all been passed around, **say:**

As you grow and change, it's important to stay con- **◁THE POINT** nected to home and family. The times you spend learning and growing with friends are among the best you can ever have. Please don't ever forget where you came from.

Close with a time for students to pray together, thanking God for the memories they have with their families and friends. Encourage teenagers to keep their paper booklets as reminders of the value in remembering their roots.

TOUGH CALLS

Work together in your group to answer each of the following questions about your youth leader to the best of your ability.

 What does your leader believe about involvement in political causes?

 What is your leader's favorite flavor of ice cream?

 How would your youth leader answer the following question: What is the proper age for teenagers to begin dating?

 What was your leader's childhood nickname?

 What is your leader's favorite song?

 According to your youth leader, what is the best style of music to listen to?

 What color shoes is your leader wearing today?

 What was your leader's first apartment or home away from home like?

CHANGED 4 LIFE

A few weeks after this study, be sure to check in with teenagers to see whether they've met with their groups from Lesson 1 and completed their life codes. Over the next several months, ask some of the teenagers to share with the group how creating a life code has impacted their lives.

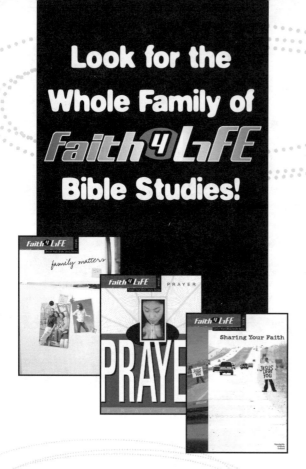